The Wonder World of Ants

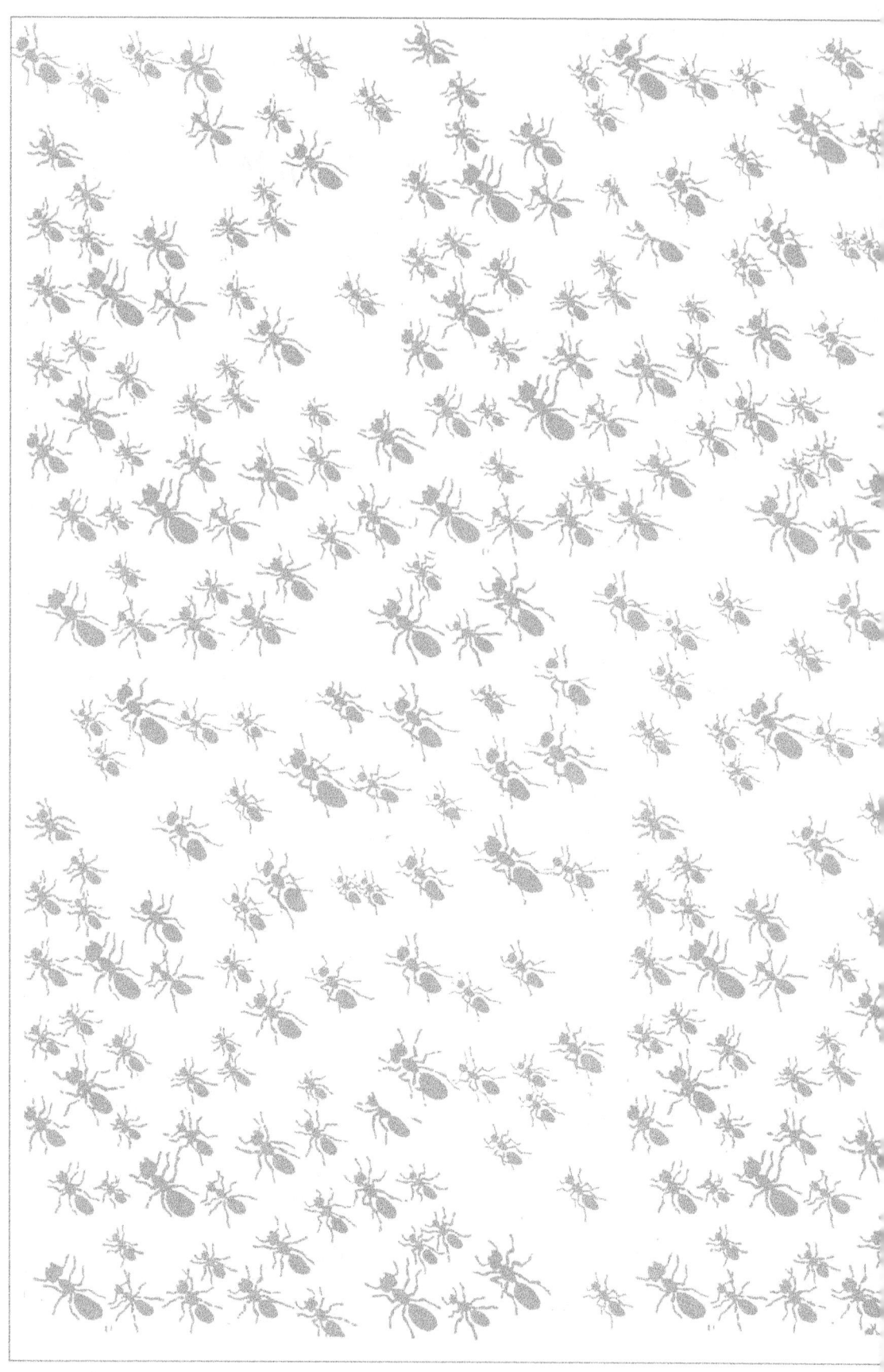

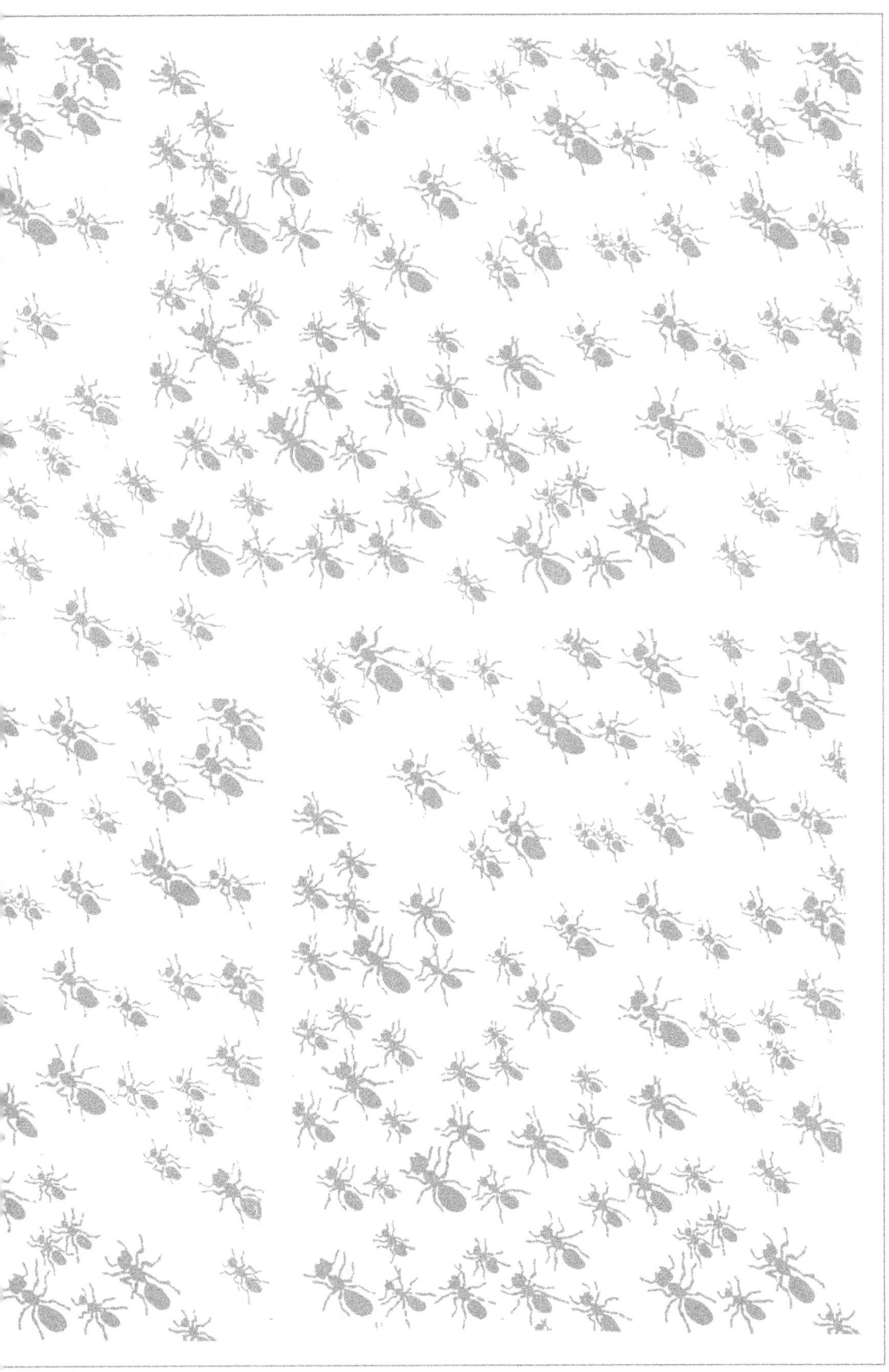

The
WONDER
WORLD
of ANTS

Wilfrid S. Bronson

Sunstone Press
SANTA FE

© 2008 by John Lounsbery. All Rights Reserved.

No part of this book may be reproduced in any form or by any electronic or mechanical means including information storage and retrieval systems without permission in writing from the publisher, except by a reviewer who may quote brief passages in a review.

Sunstone books may be purchased for educational, business, or sales promotional use. For information please write: Special Markets Department, Sunstone Press, P.O. Box 2321, Santa Fe, New Mexico 87504-2321.

Library of Congress Cataloging-in-Publication Data

Bronson, Wilfrid S. (Wilfrid Swancourt), 1894-
  The wonder world of ants / written and illustrated by Wilfrid Swancourt Bronson. -- Large print ed.
    p. cm.
  Originally published: New York : Harcourt, Brace and Company, 1937.
  ISBN 978-0-86534-691-8 (softcover : alk. paper)
  1. Ants--Juvenile literature. I. Title.
  QL568.F7B76 2008
  595.79'6--dc22
                             2008031550

WWW.SUNSTONEPRESS.COM
SUNSTONE PRESS / POST OFFICE BOX 2321 / SANTA FE, NM 87504-2321 /USA
(505) 988-4418 / ORDERS ONLY (800) 243-5644 / FAX (505) 988-1025

CONTENTS

WATCHING ANTS	3
WHAT IS AN ANT?	15
HOME BUILDERS	25
HARVESTERS	34
MUSHROOM FARMERS	41
CATTLE KEEPERS	49
HONEY SAVERS	56
BEGGARS, BOOTLEGGERS, BANDITS	62
SLAVE MAKERS	70
ARMY ANTS	80

WATCHING ANTS

WHEN I was a boy I wanted to go to Africa and see wild animals and the wild dark people as they live in Nature. But of course I could not go. So I had to pretend that I was there. Since I could not go to Africa, I went out into the fields and lay with my eyes very close to the ground, staring for hours between the weeds and grass blades. I was not a boy watching ants but an explorer. The ants were naked savages in a vast and mighty jungle.

Sometimes I saw them on safari, marching in long single files, each one carrying a precious burden as the tribe moved to some new camping ground. I visited their villages and went with them on their hunting trips. A June-bug now became an elephant; a cut-worm was a monstrous snake. A cricket was an antelope crashing through the underbrush, while grasshoppers climbing grass blades were gorillas in bamboo.

But watching ants is good fun even without pretending anything. They are very interesting insects. Scientists have studied them for many years. They have found at least eight thousand different kinds of ants. For ants are common in almost every country. And just as the people of different countries have various ways of living and looking, so do the ants. Ants are divided into na-

WATCHING ANTS

tions too, and I'm sorry to say they sometimes make war upon each other as people do. Two ant nations may want to use the same ground in which to build their cities. One nation may want to enslave another. Or it may be that they fight just because they do not understand or like each other.

As among people, ants have many ways of getting their living. There are hunter ants who capture other insects, shepherd ants who care for little bugs from which they get sweet honeydew to live on as we get milk from cows and goats. There are farmer ants who grow all their own vegetables. There are thief ants who live entirely by stealing; and slave-making ants who kidnap the children of other ant nations to do all their work. And there are mighty wandering tribes of military ants who live by plunder and make war on every living creature in their path, driving even men and elephants before them.

Ants make their homes of earth, stones, wood, paper, or leaves. We make our cellars in the earth, we bake bricks of clay, we build in stone and wood, we paper our walls. The walls themselves are only paper in Japan. Men roof their homes with a thatch of leaves in hot countries.

The very tiny Pharaoh ants may have their home right in your house. They have climbed aboard ships and traveled all over the world from Egypt. They find the weather warm enough to suit their tropical taste inside our heated houses, and help themselves in our pantries. I hope you will see no big black carpenter-ants in your house. They might be gnawing tunnels in the beams and that is very harmful. But mostly they use old dead trees to tunnel out their nests.

If you will go into the fields and turn over a few big stones, you are sure to uncover a city of ant people. You will see the workers who gather food for themselves and all the others, and the nurses who care for the baby ants. You will see some of the babies, too, though perhaps not all of them. Some may be in rooms deeper down in

WATCHING ANTS

the earth. While ant babies grow they change their form three times. First they are very small white eggs. When they hatch they are like little, very fat, white worms.

The babies you are sure to see are the ones which are wrapped in silk cocoons. People call these "ant eggs." But they are not. They are cocoons in which the baby ants are changing from fat little worms to grown-up ants. When the time comes, the cocoons will be torn open by the ant nurses, and the new ants with their tender legs and bodies very gently helped out. You may see some of these new ants, still very pale in color. They will act quite helpless in the scramble that begins when you lift the stone. They won't be strong enough to work until the skin on their jointed bodies thickens and hardens into good stout armor. The workers and nurses carry them and all the cocoons down tunnels out of sight.

If you are lucky you may see the Queen. She is much larger than her people and the hind half of her is enormous. It is full of the eggs she is forever laying. Every ant, young or old in that ant town, is a child of hers. She lays all the eggs. It is her full-time job. The nurses keep her very clean, washing her with their tongues. They take the eggs as they are laid and tend them in rooms that are warm and dry. From outside in the great world, the workers bring in food to her, and all the people seem to love her very much. She may live for fifteen years, but when she dies the whole city gradually dies out. There are no more babies being born. None of the workers can have children. And without their Queen-mother they hardly care to live themselves.

If it is not too late in the summer you may see princes and princesses in among the hustling workers. You can tell them because they have wings and bigger, better eyes than the workers. In spring and mid-summer it is their task to leave home and start new cities far and wide. On a certain day all of them must go forth. They fly

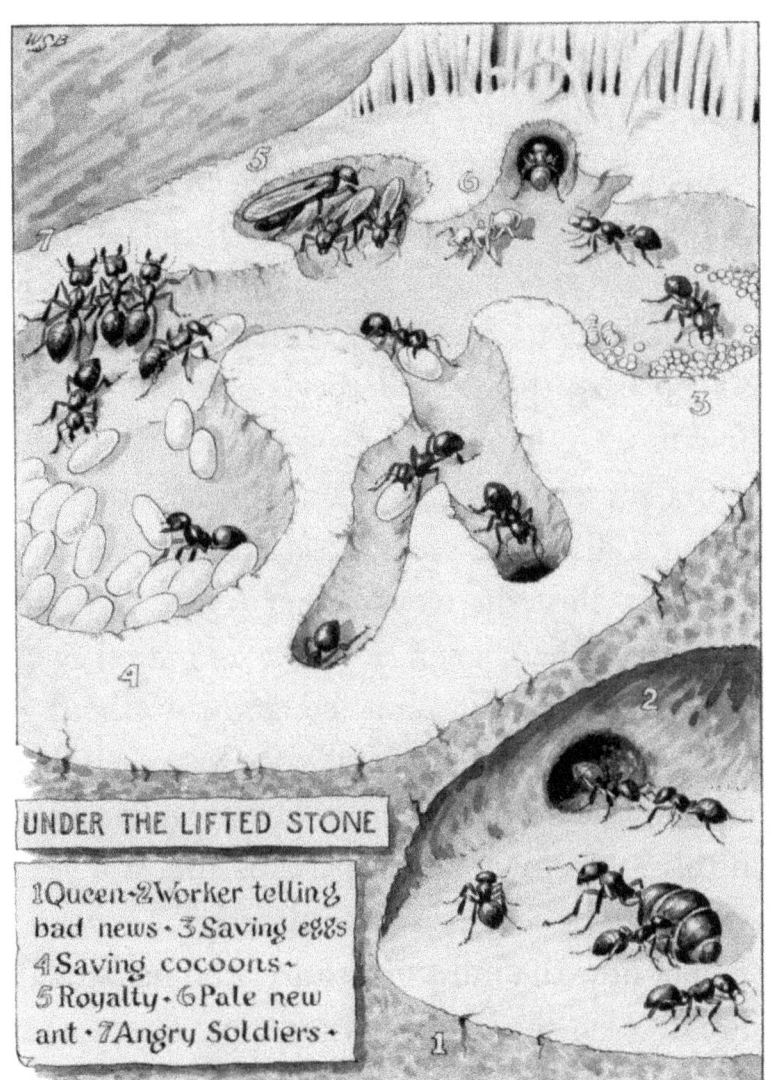

high in the air where, with their fine eyes, they see the princes and princesses from other cities of their kind. With these they mate, still flying, then separate and descend to earth again. The princes are very stupid fellows. The workers always looked after them at home. But they may not go back there. And they don't know even how to feed themselves. So they die.

But the princesses, the new Queens, they are splendid. Each one seeks a place to start her own new city. First she bites off her wings. She will never need them again. It is like taking off one's coat to go to work. With feet and jaws she digs under a log or stone, hollows out a room and then stops up the door with earth. She must live alone in this room for months, perhaps almost a year, with no food. She has been well fed all her young life but now she must live entirely on her stored-up fat. Soon she begins laying eggs. She washes them with her tongue. When the worm-like infants hatch she feeds them with her oily spittle.

WATCHING ANTS

She may lay more eggs and feed some to the babies. She may even eat a few to keep alive. She is getting thinner and thinner. After a while the babies spin cocoons. In a few weeks their mother helps them out, new, weak, underfed, runty little ants. They must still be fed until their outsides toughen, a few weeks more. At last they break open the door and go out to look for food. They bring some back to their poor and hungry mother. She gets strong again. She grows fat and lays more and better eggs. The next ants to hatch will be bigger, healthier fellows. The city will soon be full of happy, strong, hard-working people who will tunnel out new streets and apartments and make things hum.

Not all the people go out for food. Some may have extra powerful jaws. These act as guards and soldiers in time of trouble. Some workers keep the tunnels and rooms clean. All rubbish is carried out and thrown on an ants' trash heap. Some attend the Queen. And some care for the young, feeding them and moving them from room to room as they need more heat or air or moisture.

All live on liquid food. Even when they eat another insect they chew it up, suck the blood, and spit out the rest. Many kinds of ants milk the little bugs called ant-cows. They tend them with great care, placing them where they can suck plenty of sweet sap from the stems and leaves of plants. You can see them on the stems of many wild flowers and on rose bushes. These cow-bugs drink much more sap than they can use. It passes right through their bodies, only getting a little thicker and sweeter. The ants know how to make them give out delicious drops. They stroke a cow-bug's back with forelegs and feelers. The cow-bug seems to enjoy this, and presently a glistening drop of honeydew-milk appears. The ant laps it up and goes to the next cow-bug.

The ant is not gathering this food for itself alone. It uses but a little of it. It has two stomachs in its body, one for itself and one for carrying food to "the folks back home," a stomach that belongs to all the people. Almost all its hinder body is used for this. When it returns a nurse ant which has been busy indoors all day is sure to ask for honeydew. They place their mouths together. The one which has the honeydew brings up a drop from its public stomach and passes it into the nurse ant's mouth. This is how the whole city is fed. The nurse will give some of her drop to the babies, or to the Queen.

When one ant wants food from another it taps gently on the other's head with its feelers, using their telegraph code. They talk a great deal by this means. Much of the work is talked over. Perhaps one ant needs another's help in dragging home a heavy prize. If you watch long enough you will see many problems settled by this tap-talking with the feelers.

Thus go the daily doings in one ant town, such as you may find under many a stone down in the deep jungle of the fields. If you will put the stone back just the way you found it the ant townspeople will soon set things to rights again.

 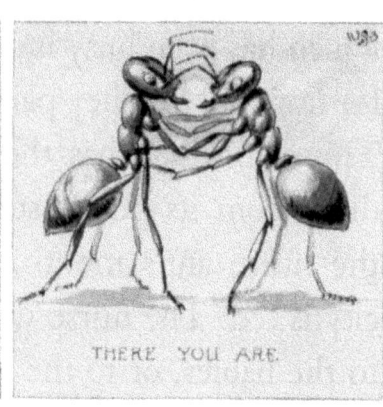

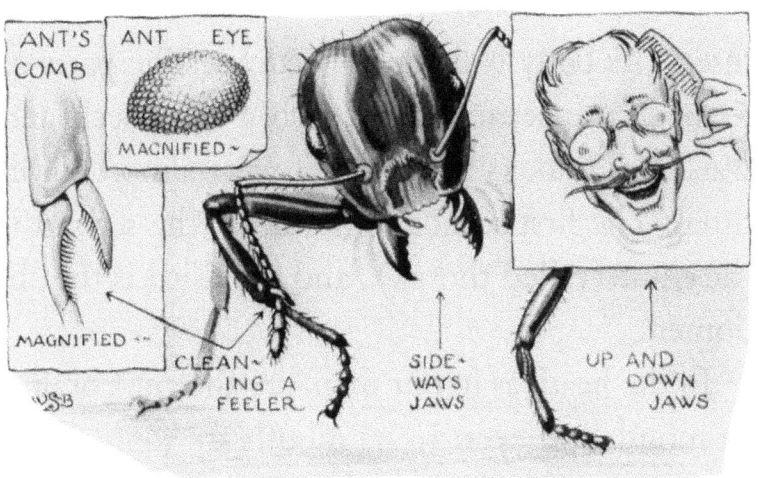

WHAT IS AN ANT?

BEFORE this book is ended we must find out about some of the very special kinds of ants living in different parts of the world. But first we ought to know a little more about what it is that makes an ant so antlike, and what makes it so much like ourselves.

An ant is like us because it is alive. It can run and see and feel. It breathes, gets hungry, builds a home and brings up children. But an ant is an insect. Its body is made in sections. The parts of its body are separated by such a thin neck and waist that it looks as though it were almost cut in three. The first section is the head, the second is the chest (called thorax), and the third is the abdomen.

In the head, as in our own, are the ant's brains, its mouth and eyes. In its mouth are tongue and jaws. But instead of working up and down as ours do, the ant's jaws move from each side to the middle. The eyes are rather different from our own. They are made up of many smaller eyes and cannot be rolled about as ours can. We view a horse standing still just as readily as a horse galloping. If the horse is still, our eyes move very quickly all over him. We get a good idea of his shape. But when an ant looks at a resting grasshopper its eyes cannot move to view it thoroughly. The ant's idea of what the hopper looks like is much more clear when the hopper moves a little.

WHAT IS AN ANT?

On the head also are the ant's two noses, the feelers used for smelling. They also serve as fingers, the ant touching whatever interests it to learn its nature through the feel. But these are not its only fingers. Growing out of its chest section, the ant has (instead of two arms) six legs. Often it uses its front feet as we use our hands, to touch things, to grasp them, to lift, to push and pull. And its jaws are also used for grasping, lifting, pushing and pulling. So we might say the ant has fingers all over its face and chest.

On the back of their chest section some ants have wings. These are the royalty, the young princes and princesses at the beginning of their lives as grown-ups. The long lacy wings of a princess ant are like the filmy veil a bride wears to her wedding and removes forever once she is married and queen of her own new home. As we have seen, the princess ant flies to her wedding and takes off her wings when she is ready to start a home and family of her own.

THE WONDER WORLD OF ANTS

In the third section, the abdomen, are an ant's two stomachs, one much larger than the other. The small one is for its own use. The large one is a shopping bag in which it brings home food for other ants. In the drawing you will see how different are the sizes of its private and public stomachs.

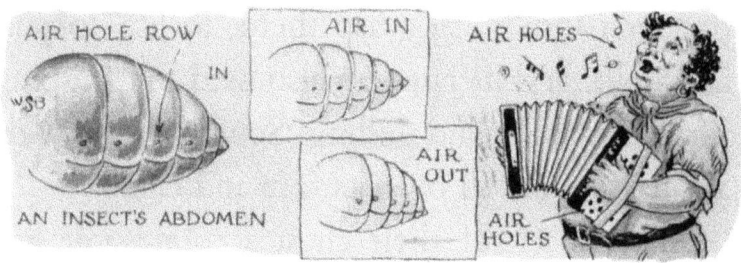

An ant has jointed legs and so do we. But the ant's joints are on the outside while ours are inside. The hard armor worn by the ant is its only skeleton, it has no bones. "In days of old when knights were bold" they imitated insects with the metal armor which they wore. A knight oiled his armor to keep it from rusting and squeaking. The tidy ant shines its armor often with its oily saliva. For that matter, many people

WHAT IS AN ANT?

use olive oil to clean their skins. Many use oily cold-creams, and in Africa a woman will put rancid butter on her head, letting it melt down over her body. The knight breathed through his helmet, but the ant breathes through two rows of holes in the sides of its armor. Tubes carry the air from these holes into all parts of its body for it has no lungs. When we breathe in, our lungs swell like toy balloons, and shrink as the air goes out again. Ants breathe by moving their abdomens like accordions. You can notice this more easily by watching the ant's bigger relative, the wasp.

Before oiling itself an ant removes dust from its head and feelers. For this it has a fine pair of combs on each foreleg. The teeth of the combs meet and the feeler is pulled between them. But whereas we may remove a stray hair from a comb with our fingers, the ant must clean its combs in its jaws.

All through our bodies we have nerves, but the

THE WONDER WORLD OF ANTS

biggest ones are in our backs. The ant's big nerves run down its under side. The heart of an ant, instead of being in its chest, is in the middle of its back.

Though ants work very hard they take time to play sometimes. They wrestle with each other and may roll a grain of wheat around for the same fun we take in playing ball. There are ants which stop their work to gather as at a great convention. They all sit gently waving their feelers, which may be the way they listen at a meeting. No one knows how ants hear. Their "ears" have never been found. Perhaps the feelers are not only noses and fingers, but ears as well. Maybe they are like portable radio receiving sets. At least we know the ants do hear, but what the meetings are about is still a mystery.

The meetings may have something to do with the government of their ant country to which all are very loyal. Just as the ant's public stomach is much larger than its own, so it cares more for

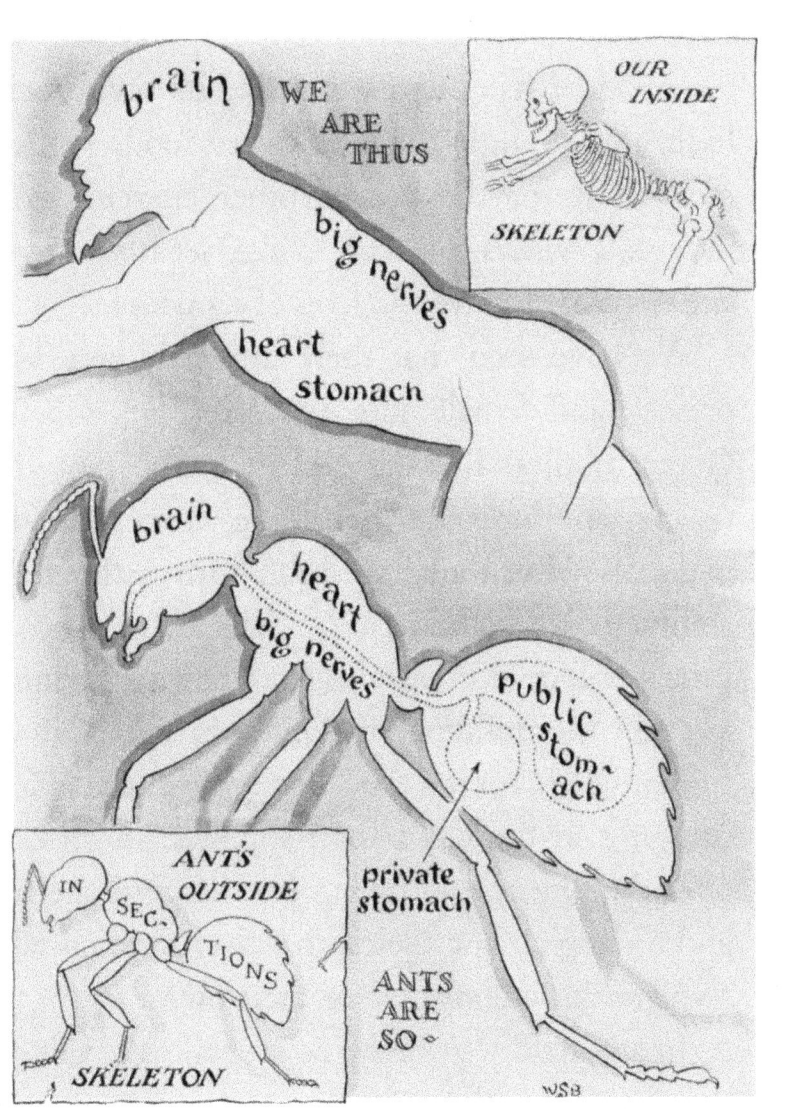

the good of its country than for its own good. Each ant, though fond of sweet food, gathers most of it for the use of other citizens. And though it wishes to go on living, yet it will fight and even die to save the lives of its people.

We have seen that there are male ants, the princes, and female ants, the princesses and the Queen-mother. But the greatest number of ants that swarm through the city, the workers, are females also. But they have been born without the ability to have children of their own. And so probably they do not wish to. They are so interested in the building of their great cities, in all the endless chores to be done, in hunting and bringing in the city's food supplies, in looking after the Queen and caring for the eggs she lays and rearing all her babies, that they have no wish to be raising youngsters of their own.

In any field there may be several different ant nations. A number of cities may belong to one nation if their Queens are sisters. One ant can tell

WHAT IS AN ANT?

another's nationality by its smell. All ants of one nation smell the same. Ants which do not smell alike are foreigners to each other, and may be enemies. Each nation claims a certain region as its land and no other kind of ant is supposed to trespass there. They do not put up "No trespassing, no hunting" signs, but they have scouts who patrol the border. These use a trespasser very badly. Or should a whole nation of enemy ants be about to trespass to attack the scouts' own cities, they rush home to give the alarm. There is no time to tell each citizen by feeler tap-talking. They bang their heads against the walls of their tunnels as we might strike a fire-bell. It is just as though they shouted, "Call out the guard!" Everybody knows at once what is wrong and they get ready to fight off the attack.

Of all insects ants are no doubt the smartest. Thousands of them, united, form great nations, with a very useful language, and a government, vast numbers of hard-working people and their own armies of soldiers. The smartest animals which have backbones and inside skeletons are men. And men have nations, language, government, vast numbers of working people and armies. This is true of only ants and men. So now let us go on a travel tour in the world of ants to learn the ways of their various nations, scattered as the nations of men, over the whole face of the earth.

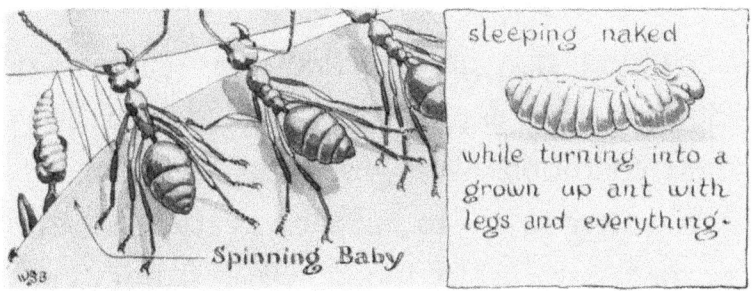

HOME BUILDERS

ONLY a few rooms, a very small part of the ant tribe's home, was uncovered when you raised the stone that was their roof. You watched worried workers hastily removing all cocoons which lay in the warm, dry, well-aired rooms you had exposed. Those cocoons just happened to need some warm dry air the day you came along. The nurses had brought them to the upper rooms where the warm sun toasted the stone. Even if you had not disturbed them they would probably have taken their precious bundles to rooms down deeper in the ground, which do not cool so quickly, after the sun has set. Other ant children may have needed moist coolness on that day. They lay in rooms still deeper down where conditions were just right for them.

Ants have rooms to suit their every need. Cool dry rooms, warm dry rooms, warm damp rooms, cool damp rooms. According to what the babies need the nurses move them about, even taking them at times out into the open for an airing. If it is the home of ants which keep cows underground, there will be rooms hollowed out around the deeper roots of plants, where milkmaids work without having to set a foot outdoors. There are storerooms where collected food is kept, and rooms where rubbish is put if it is not taken immediately to the trash heap, the ants' "town dump," outside. Outside also may be the ant cemetery. For some ants bury their dead, though other kinds simply carry them away.

No room belongs to any ant alone. All the rooms belong to all the people, to be used as needed, except one room. The Queen's chamber

"SAWDUST"

CARPENTER ANTS AT WORK

← If you could slice the old tree down its middle · · · · · ·

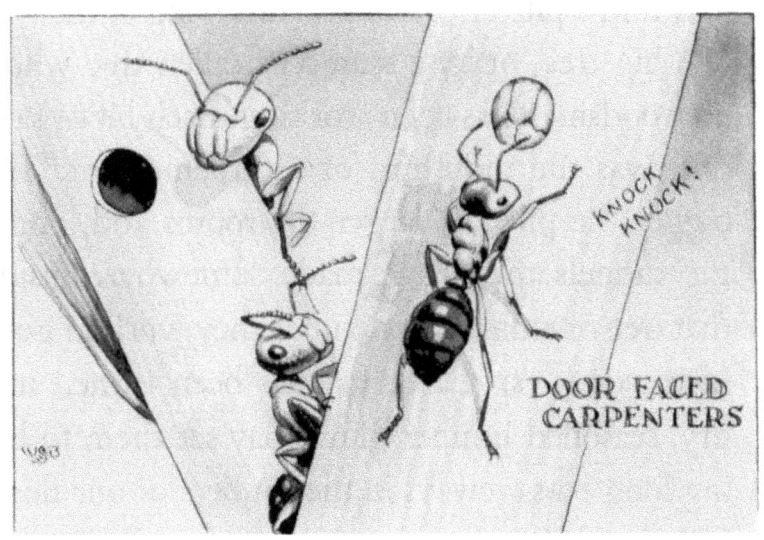

KNOCK KNOCK!

DOOR FACED CARPENTERS

is for her use only. Other ants are there as attendants, guards and nurses, but it is a special room for a particularly special ant. It is a place as sacred to the ants as the village church is to the people of its congregation. In that room each ant was born in an egg laid by its revered Queen-mother.

Carpenter ants work in wood. Instead of hollowing out their hallways in the earth they bite their way into the softened parts of old trees. You may find a pile of coarse sawdust lying at the base of a big tree, or by a stump or fallen tree where no woodsman has been working. Each bit of sawdust was the mouthful of a carpenter ant. The bigger the pile the larger the rooms and longer the tunnels they have made somewhere inside that tree or stump. Sometimes they work in good firm wood, especially if it has been turned into dry, seasoned lumber. This may set them to biting long passageways in the timbers of our floors and walls. Their sawdust may be piled somewhere we never see, say in a dark corner of the coal bin.

When I was four years old my mother's cousin came to visit. She weighed two hundred pounds. One day she went to carry a big hamper full of clothes down into the cellar laundry. She was very strong and set me atop the clothes for a ride. Half way down she sank through the stairs. I coasted in the basket to the bottom in high glee. But my cousin was calling for help. It wasn't the splinters she minded so much. When they got her out of the stairs they found the beams all tunneled through and swarming with angry, biting, big black carpenter ants!

Another kind of carpenter ant bores into the stems of stout sedge grasses. Their soldiers have hard faces for extra guard duty. The front of these faces fits exactly into the circular openings made in the sedge stems, which are used as doors. In every opening a soldier's tough muzzle blocks the way completely. It cannot see out. But nothing can go in without its permission. A worker comes home, perhaps tired and carrying a load of booty. But before she may enter she must knock to be admitted. Her odor and her tap-talk prove she really "lives at that address." The soldier backs out of the way, lets her pass, and again plugs the door with its muzzle.

In South America certain ants make "flower-ball" homes in jungle trees. The trees are very tall, the jungle deep and dimly lit save high up where the sun shines over it. A part of each year the jungle floor is very wet and often flooded. So the ants choose to live in the shaded region half way up the trees. There are certain flowering plants which cannot live in floods nor in the glaring sun that strikes the jungle top. It is with these plants and mud that the ants make their beautiful homes. From the ground, one mouthful at a time, the mud is carried up and plastered about a branch till a ball about the size of your head is formed. Then the seeds of these special

HOME BUILDERS

plants are gathered and planted in the mud ball. They sprout and the roots spread through the ball binding it all together. Then when the tropical rains come the ball does not wash away. But the plants burst into bloom. The ants need not worry about the floods below. Their rooms are snug amongst the flower-ball roots. They live in the beauty of their garden city far up above the troubled earth.

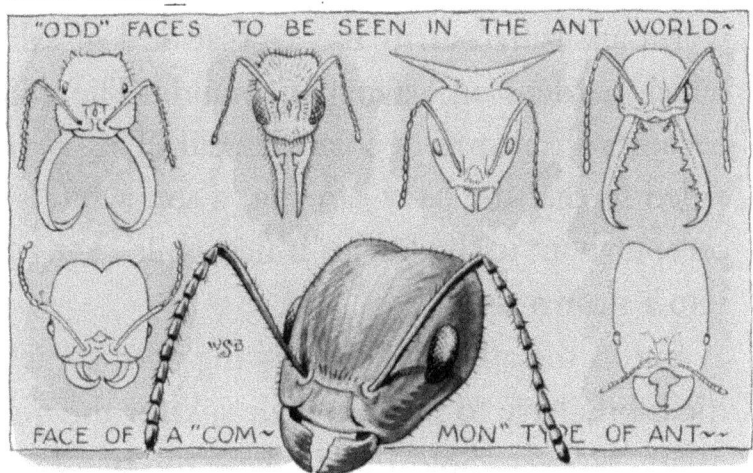

Another kind of tropical ant which lives in jungle trees makes rooms of silk and living leaves. A place is selected where a number of leaves grow close enough to each other to be pulled together until they touch. To bring them together a number of ants make a rope of themselves, each one clinging to the next. They hold fast to the upper leaf while ants on the lower leaf pull. When the two leaves touch, other ants hold them fast while still others start sewing them together. Here is where the children help. Grown-up ants cannot spin silk from their mouths. But every little white worm ant baby can. It has a great deal of saliva which hardens on leaving its mouth. The saliva becomes a transparent silken thread. This is provided so that the baby can spin a soft white silk cocoon about itself. In this it lies while changing into a grown-up.

But in the affairs of leaf-sewing ants, some of the babies have to give up their silk for the good of all. Workers hold them where the two leaves are being pulled together, and without complaining, the babies let their silk saliva flow. First its mouth is touched to one leaf, then to the other.

HOME BUILDERS

Back and forth the worker moves the spinning baby, adding thread to thread until the leaves hold and the other workers may let go. This is done wherever they plan to fit the edges of leaves together. Once the outside is finished, more babies are used to spin a silken lining for the inside. In there all the babies who gave up their silk have to lie naked while they change to grown-ups. It is as though they were lying in a hospital ward instead of a private room. There are the nurses going from one to another, and there are the various visitors. These ants make many such rooms in trees. They are honey cow-keepers and build leaf and silken barns to keep their cattle in. And the babies must spin for these as well.

HARVESTERS

WE said in the beginning that scientists have studied the ants for many years. To them we owe much of what we know about ants. But all sorts of people have studied them for thousands of years and each has looked on what he saw in his own way, just as you will. Common men and kings, poets, philosophers and artists, all tell us things about the ants. Sometimes the things they tell contradict each other. Scientists disagree with other scientists just as often as they pooh-pooh the ideas of, perhaps, a poet who writes of ants. But sometimes a poet

HARVESTERS

or an artist will see what the scientist may not. He will watch an ant do something most remarkable which seemingly only a very wise creature would *think* of doing. But some scientist may say that ants don't think, that they do as they do because they are as they are, and can't think of any other way to do what they do. And so it goes and has gone on for many hundreds of years.

Great King Solomon was sure the ants were wise and said so about three thousand years ago. He advised some people of his kingdom to be less lazy and to think of the future. He said, "Go to the ant, thou sluggard, consider her ways and be wise. . . . She provideth her meat in the summer, and gathereth her food in the harvest." That great ruler had taken time to watch the ants bringing in dead insects and the seeds of grasses and grain to store up for the wintertime when food is scarce.

King Solomon almost surely was watching the harvester ants which live near desert places in the

Old World. Here in the New World we have their relatives on the western prairies and the dry plains of states like Texas. They pile up enormous mounds of dirt while digging out their underground cities, for their populations are tremendous. This is possible because they live for the most part on seeds. They like meat but they are never sure of a supply in the dry and desert places where they live. So they do not count on it but live as vegetarians mostly.

It is almost always easier to supply more vegetables than meat. Can you imagine how it would be if everyone in New York City stopped eating anything but meat? The cattle, sheep, pig and poultry supply would soon give out. But if the people only wanted vegetables, the supply could be kept up year after year. So it is with the big cities of harvester ants. When grass seeds are ripe they take them to their granaries to save against hard times. They go to the grain fields of prairie farmers too, and help themselves, harvesting a

HARVESTERS

crop they did not sow.

One quarrel among the scientists is about whether the harvester ants plant any crops of their own. They are very fond of the seeds of a grass called Aristida, and bring home much of it from far afield. Quite often they have a small crop of it growing close by. All scientists agree that the ants planted this near-by patch. But some say "on purpose," some say "by accident." Those who say "on purpose" argue that these ants know a lot about the seeds they use. They know what to do about stored seeds which start to sprout. The sprouts are allowed to grow a little, then bitten off and the seeds then dried in the sun. This sprouting and sunning makes them sweeter. The "on purpose" scientists will say that an ant which knows enough to do this will also know that a seed which has sprouted too far is no good for eating anymore, and that it will carry the seed to a place where it can take root and grow to produce more seeds.

The "by accident" scientists will say that of course the ants know what is no longer good to eat and that they always take useless things out onto the trash heap, which is right where this grass crop always grows—the seeds are simply thrown away, but some of them take root.

The trash heap is at the edge of a broad space kept clean by the harvesters all about their mounded city. From it the good ant roads lead away to the harvest fields. No grass or weed is allowed to grow on them, no litter is allowed to

HARVESTERS

lie. The workers bring their loads in over smooth highways. Other workers stay in the fields, climbing the grasses, snipping off the seeds and sometimes whole ears of seeds at once. At the city entrances still other workers receive what the carriers bring. They tear off the husks and turn the seeds over to small workers who carry them down to the dry storerooms. These rooms may be five inches wide and have been found down seven feet underground. Then there are the miller workers who make some of the grain into flour. Their heads are very large because of the powerful muscles which move their great grinding jaws. They crunch the seeds into a kind of "whole-wheat" flour and some of the harvesters even bake bread of it. They mix their spittle with the flour and roll up little dough balls the size of peppercorns. These they bake in the sun and store away.

Harvester ants are not warlike but it does not pay to pester them. Their bite is poisonous. It makes men sick and dizzy, and it will quickly kill a mouse. There are numerous varieties of harvester ants and some of them wear beards, a fringe of hairs about their faces. The bearded harvester ants of Texas have one unconquerable enemy. This is the little horned toad which is really a lizard. Its scales are covered with horny spines, a tough armor through which no ant can bite. So there are times of great trouble in a harvester city when a horned toad comes calling and eats up many of the people.

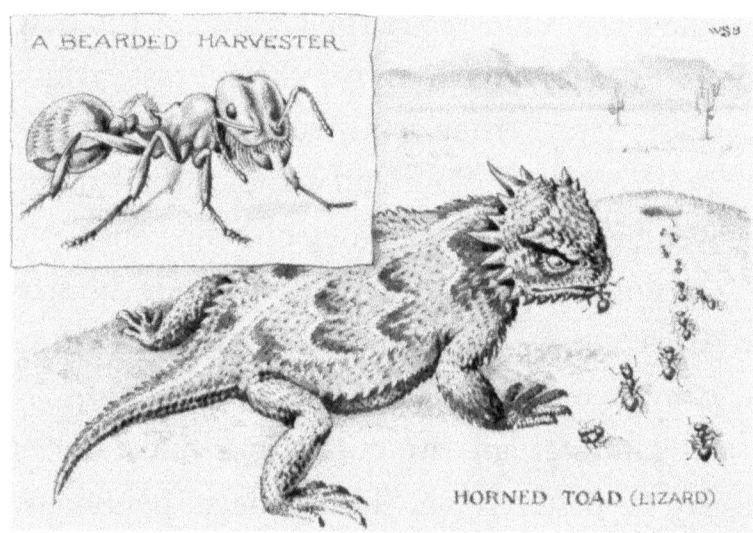

MUSHROOM FARMERS

THERE is doubt as to whether harvester ants plant Aristida grass. But there is no doubt about the ants which live on mushrooms. For one thing, the kind of mushrooms they eat grows nowhere else at all but in the cellars of these ants. Besides, they have been carefully watched at their farming. They are a people who grow all the food they ever use right in town, for they eat nothing but their own especially home-grown mushrooms. This makes possible the biggest ant cities on earth. The more people, the more mushroom cellars, the more mushrooms, the more people. Their city may be as big as half a block of our own cities, and may be dug down as deep as five or six yards underground.

Think of the number of ants that can live in

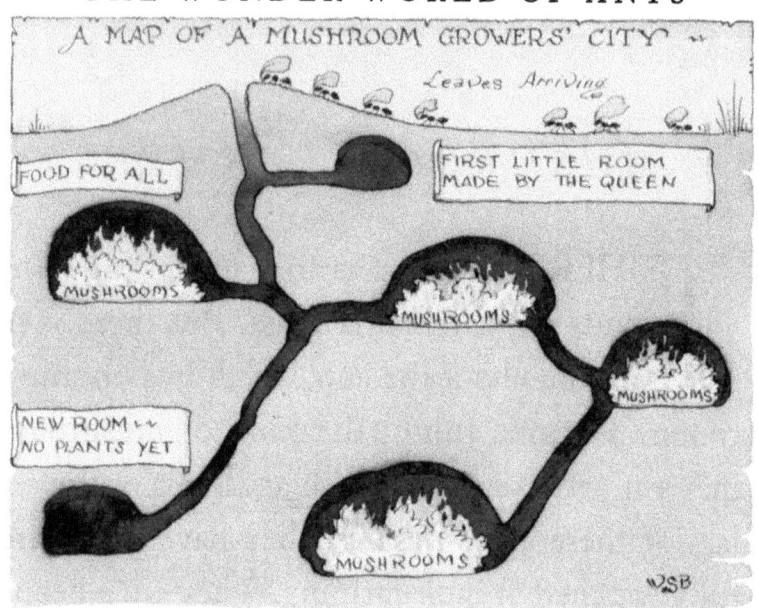

half a man-size city block. Think of the vast supply of mushrooms they must eat. Think of the tremendous amount of fertilizer they must gather to keep the mushrooms growing. The ants make the fertilizer out of leaves which they chew into a paste and stick either on the floors or ceilings of their cellars. On this leaf paste the mushrooms grow. These gardens have to be weeded, for other kinds of mushrooms try to grow there which the ants don't want. And the mushrooms

MUSHROOM FARMERS

have to be pruned constantly. If not they would grow to be big mushrooms like those men eat. The ants do not want this either. They keep clipping off the shooting stems and presently the plant, held back this way, produces round swellings which glisten like bright clustered drops of water. These are the parts eaten.

The underground work of these insect farmers is wonderful to think about, but the above ground work they do is amazing to behold. You realize what an enormous lot of leaves must be used to fertilize the mushrooms. The ants cannot plant a bed on leaf paste and call it finished. Every so often they must prepare new paste and throw away the old. So thousands of them go forth to gather fresh leaves. Each cuts a piece two or three times the size of its body and presently you may see them returning home in a long line, each like a lady with a big umbrella. They are often spoken of as parasol ants. It is something like a fashionable summer Sunday of other days, with many ladies on parade under their parasols.

The ants need so many leaves that they often strip every one from a tree. This is very bad for any man who is trying to raise oranges. If the ants decide that the leaves of his trees will give them a good mushroom crop, they prevent him from harvesting any fruit crop at all. Tropical fruit farmers have to try to get rid of these little mushroom farmers, but it is not at all easy. Much of the ants' home is so deep in the ground that though men dig great holes and burn fires in them and have blowers to push the smoke through the ant tunnels and rooms, it very often doesn't work. The Queen's chamber may not get any of the smoke and lots of the rooms never do. Though things may quiet down for a while, before long the ants are back for more of the farmer's leaves.

Of course they do not know that the trees belong to him. They only know that on those trees are just the right leaves for their mushrooms. So,

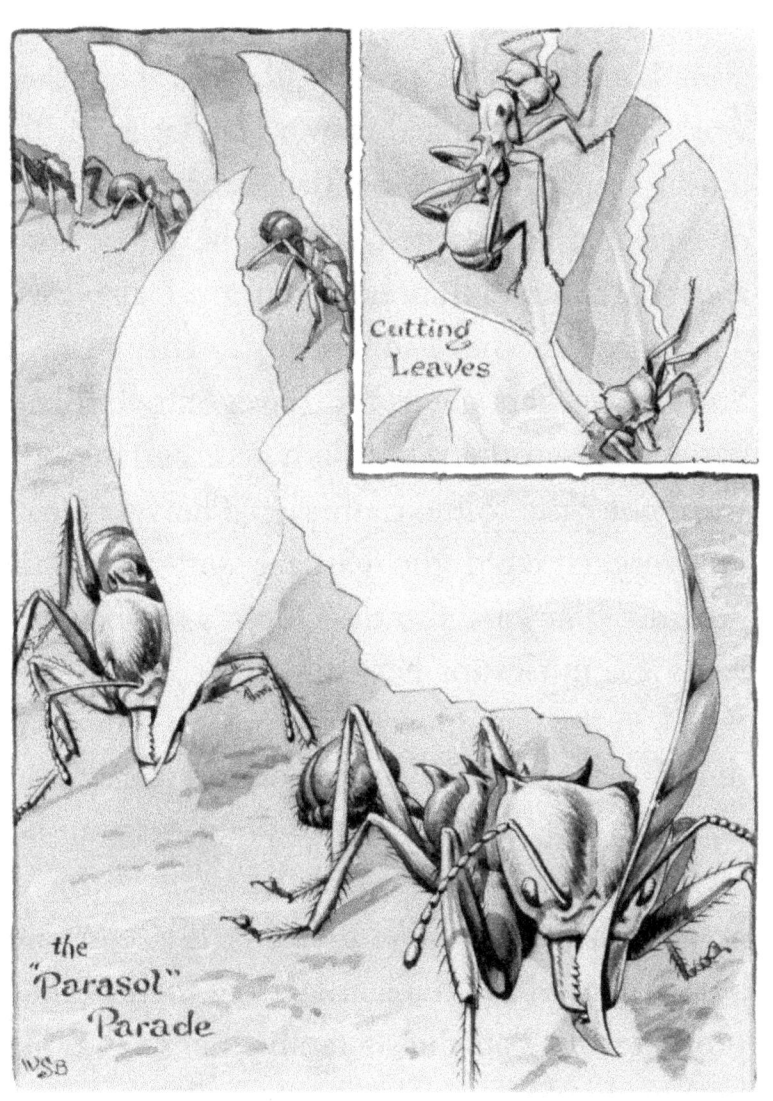

even though they are stealing, they go about their work in an unhurried way. The tasks of the mushroom farmers are divided amongst a variety of workers. The largest are on the police force and guard the entrances to the great ant town. The medium sized ones go for the leaves. Smaller workers chew the leaves into fertilizer paste, put it in the mushroom beds and take the worn out paste to the trash pile. The very smallest workers weed the gardens and prune the growths. They are also the Queen's personal servants and nurses for her children.

When the new Queens go forth to their weddings, each carries a supply of tiny mushroom plantings inside her mouth to use in starting her own city. After she has sealed herself up in the hole she has dug, she crushes her first eggs and puts the mushroom plantings on them. These grow, feeding on the "scrambled eggs." When her next batch of eggs has hatched she has to feed the babies on still other eggs till they spin themselves cocoons. When they come out as grown-ups they are not very grand to look upon, small and stunted, but they can work. The Queen no longer has to care for the eggs she keeps on laying, nor does she have to weed and clip the growing mushroom patch. She doesn't even have to wash herself any more. The new workers take good care of her and her babies and her garden. They dig out to the great wide world and dash to get leaves. No more raising mushrooms on the Queen's best eggs. From now on every egg is to be a citizen ant someday. They dig new and bigger cellars and plant more and ever more mushrooms.

For every new Queen who succeeds in starting a city, there are often many who fail. In the jungles of Brazil, Indians catch them when they come to earth after their weddings in the air, pinch off their heads, and fry their fat bodies which burst like popcorn and become very crisp. This is considered a very choice dish. Indeed, it is said that the Indian children often do not wait for the frying but eat them raw. The red man sometimes makes use of insects which are only a pest and torment to the white man.

Not all mushroom-growing ants have mighty cities. Some kinds live in small communities. I didn't tell you (in the chapter on Home Builders) that the flower-ball-making ants are some of these. Up there in their lovely blooming ball of mud those little ants are also raising mushrooms. During floods their fertilizer is still where they can get it. Up the tree they go and bring down leaves. So you see, the flower-ball gardener is a mushroom farmer too.

CATTLE KEEPERS

IN our first chapter we found out something about ant-cows and how milkmaids collect honeydew from their herds. If it is spring or summer you may have seen hundreds of the ant-cows in their pastures on the stems of dandelions and roadside weeds, or the leaves of many shrubs. Not all of them are watched by herders, though sooner or later the ants are likely to discover them and become their owners. Those watched over by the ants are much safer than when "running wild." For there are other insects which will attack them just as wolves or lions will attack man's cattle when they can.

But the ants are good herdsmen or herdsmaids. They will fight fiercely to protect their little cows. If you know of an ant-cow pasture and want to test their courage, take a dry grass stem and rub its end between your fingers. Then push it gently among the tiny cattle and watch how ferociously the herder's jaws will open to bite the grass that smells like a giant. You will see the ant-cows' calves there too. You may even see some of them being born. They are born like real calves, alive, from their mothers, for they hatch from the eggs in her body before she has time to lay them. In about two short weeks they are grown ant-cows, giving honeydew and having calves of their own.

Into the barn for winter's coming...

CATTLE KEEPERS

All summer long this goes on until the autumn when the sap they suck flows more slowly. Then other things are slower also. The little calves don't hatch so quickly. They wait inside the eggs which their mother lays. The ants gather eggs and mothers, taking them all down into their sheltered town, safe from the cold and wet of winter.

As spring comes they dig tunnels to the roots of smartweed and other early plants, hollowing out rooms around them. These rooms are their barns, for here they bring their cows, placing them on the roots to suck the juice, still sheltered from the raw spring weather. New calves hatch from the eggs saved so carefully all winter, and are placed in these barns with their mothers. By the time farmers' corn plants are up a little way the ants have tunneled to them. They hollow barns around these and move their cattle to the juicy new sweet roots. This spoils the corn plant's growth and makes the farmer as angry as you made the herder on the dandelion stalk. The ants which bother farmers most this way are known as cornfield ants and their cattle are called corn root lice. These prefer to stay underground in their cozy barns even after good warm weather comes. Other kinds of ant-cow plant lice are carried out and placed again in the places where you will find them.

When ant-cows don't give as much honeydew as the ants would like, they are taken to some other plant where more sap flows. Just as though a farmer should say to his hired man, "Casper, you'd better turn the cows into the north pasture today. South one's gettin' too short!" The farmer's cows are always glad to get into new fields, but ant-cows are hard to move. Each has a beak like a hollow needle through which it sucks the sap about as you use a straw at a soda fountain. But it is not as simple as that. For the beak is thrust deep under the bark or skin on the plant the ant-cow is living on, and pulling it free is not

CATTLE KEEPERS

like lifting a straw from your soda. The ants have to tug and work very hard sometimes to get these needle-beaks out without hurting the cows which

ANTS DO DAIRYING WITH BUGS LIKE THESE

MEN GET MILK FROM ANIMALS LIKE THESE

are very delicate and could very easily be torn to pieces with a little carelessness.

Ants have other honey-giving cows besides the plant-lice kinds. They use quite a number of different sap-sucking bugs, some of which look very odd as you can see in their pictures. There seem to be about as many kinds of bugs to give honeydew to ants as there are animals to give milk to people. In America we get our milk from cows and goats. In other lands people milk these as well as mares, sheep, camels and reindeer. And of course, new born babies have their mothers' milk before they learn to drink the other kinds. Ants take honeydew from plant-lice, root-lice, bark-lice, tree-hoppers, leaf-hoppers, mealy-bugs, and several other insects. Many of these are stroked and coaxed for their honeydew, but the ants just go among some of them, picking up small hardened drops of it where the bug-cows have let it fall.

There are places in the world where the bug-cows drop so much honeydew to harden on the leaves and ground beneath, that a person can collect several pounds of it in a day. It is as good for people as it is for ants. The wild people of Australia eat all they can get of it. When Moses was leading the Children of Israel to the Promised Land, and they had gotten lost in the wilderness, they would have starved to death if they had not found some of this food. They did not know that tiny insects had sucked it from the wilderness bushes and dropped it there, but thought it fell direct from Heaven. They needed no explanation. It was a gift from God. They called it Manna, and as such it is collected and sold and eaten in Near East countries to this very day.

HONEY SAVERS

IN the world of ants, honey is money, we might say. For though it is food, it is at the same time a form of golden wealth that passes from one to another. No ant keeps all it has and by constant exchange of riches the whole nation is fed and kept well, and mostly happy. When ants milk ant-cows for honeydew, it is like drawing wages for their labor, which keeps them alive and enables them to help feed the family. Bees of course do much better when taking nectar from flowers, for they put much of it by for later use. That's why many banks have a picture of a beehive in their decorations. But there is one kind of ant which saves its honey-money as carefully as bees.

HONEY SAVERS

Out in the dry parts of our country in the far Southwest, there are ants which have invented a different kind of bank than that of the bees. They cannot make the wax containers in which bees store their wealth, building ever bigger honeycombs. But some of the workers in each city of the honey saver ants act as bankers and also are the very banks themselves. Honey wealth is put into them and taken out as needed. When hard times come and the workers' wages are low, they go to these bank members of their community and draw whatever they need from the savings.

Only during the short wet season of each year can these ants find honeydew in plenty. Then, when desert flowers bloom, they get some of the nectar and on the stems of desert roses find their precious little cows. When the roses begin to fade and dry there is one more place to which the ants may go to gather honey. In the groves of scrubby oak trees there still are riches to be found. This is because of the work of a certain fly which uses

THE WONDER WORLD OF ANTS

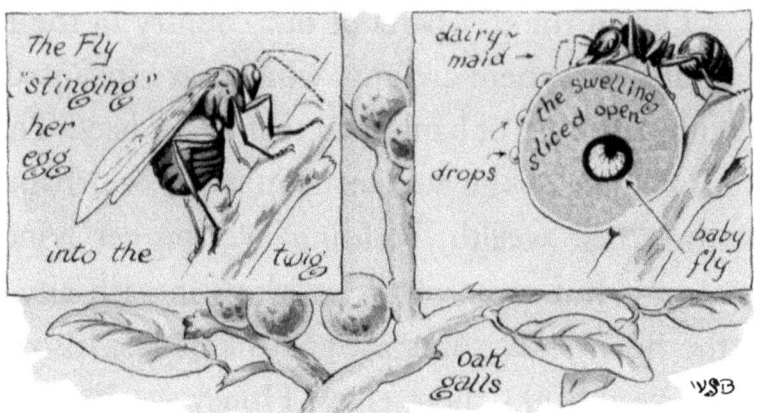

the trees as a nursery for its young ones.

The fly has an egg-layer on its rear end which is long and sharp like a sting. It is also hollow, a tube through which the fly's egg must pass when being laid. The fly sticks it into the nice juicy green wood of oak leaf stems and drops an egg down through it. The stem begins to swell very much as your finger would if stung by a wasp. When the baby fly hatches from the egg in the oak stem it lies in this swollen place in solid oaken comfort. As it soaks up the sweet sap which runs through the stem it grows and wriggles. This works like scratching a mosquito bite. The swol-

HONEY SAVERS

len place swells larger and larger around the wriggly baby, bulging out until it looks like a bright green fruit. An oyster cannot fight or run away any more than an oak tree can. To defend itself from some unwanted thing inside its shell it builds a pearl around it. Perhaps the oak builds this round green lump about the baby fly for the same reason. And the lump is as precious to the ants as the finest pearl would be to man. For through the green bark stretched tightly over the swelling, ooze many drops of honeydew sap. The ants come along, lap them up and come back later when more drops appear.

For a while the scrubby trees may be so full of green swellings that they seem to be bearing fruit instead of acorns. During this season, working only when the scorching sun has set, the Honey Savers gather every drop of honey they can find, take it back to town, feed the people, and put the rest away in their living honey-moneybags.

These honey-moneybags are certain workers

who have learned to store away more honey in their public stomachs than other workers can, steadily bulging ever bigger till they fill out round as balloons and big as grapes, chock full of honey. Of course ants so heavily laden can do no active work. They can only store the public wealth. So that becomes their calling, and their sister workers hang them on the ceiling. They "set them up" in the banking business. Side by side, in various rooms well underground, hang many of these living honey-moneybags. Their claws hook into the rough ceilings which are high enough above the smooth floor so that their bulging bodies do not touch it. This makes it easy for workers to keep the rooms clean. Others come back from honey gathering, climb up to where a bulging sister hangs and tap on her head what must mean "Open your mouth, here's more to save." The living bag swallows what the worker has brought into her public stomach where it will stay till needed later.

HONEY SAVERS

It would seem to be a very dull life hanging all the time in the darkness underground doing absolutely nothing but taking in honey or giving out a little at a time to busy hungry sisters. These bankers may hang on at their strange job for years, but at last, of course, death ends their careers. The dead ant's little claws let go and she falls to the floor. She must be removed. The honey in her public stomach is as good as ever, but the workers do not use a bit of it. It is as though they feel it to be sacred to the dead. Perhaps it could be called the honey-money she had saved for funeral expenses. At any rate, the workers have to cut her in two, taking the forward half, the head, thorax and legs, away to a burial place and then rolling the dead honey-moneybag, her abdomen, to a place set aside for such things. They could never move their dead sister through the tunnels all in one piece.

Southwestern Indians gather swollen honey ants to eat, and so do wild men in the arid regions of Australia.

BEGGARS, BOOTLEGGERS, BANDITS

GREAT King Solomon urged his people to be more like the industrious ant. Probably he did not know that in the ant world there are loafers and evil doers, just as in the world of men. Indeed, not only are there wicked ant-world persons who commit crimes, but whole nations of ants which live entirely by begging from or robbing other ants. Doing little or no work themselves, they steal food from working nations, even taking the children and, cannibals that they are, gobbling them up as special tidbits.

BEGGARS, BOOTLEGGERS, BANDITS

You remember that the harvester ants keep a wide court swept clean all about the entrance to their city. If Solomon had had more time for natural history he might one day have found a harvester city whose courtyard was not so neat. Here and there it would be sullied by the holes and hills of another smaller kind of ant. Solomon might have seen a gang of these small ants waiting along the smooth highway till a harvest worker toiled homeward with a heavy load of food. He would have seen them jump upon her from all sides, biting her till she let go of the food to defend herself, the fruits of her toil being dragged into the den of the robbers. And this new wisdom would have made him sad perhaps. For he would know that while people are no worse than ants, the ants are no better than people. They are really as much alike as he was urging them to be.

Harvesters are often pestered by these petty plunderers and after a while when their patience is gone, they do something about it. Now, earthworms eat decaying plants. Therefore they like to live under the harvesters' rubbish heap where so much chaff and so many spoiled seeds are piled. Even though the climate is hot and dry, the ground is always moist under the rubbish and pleasant for the worms. It is the earthworm's job in life to turn dead and dying plants into good rich earth again. If you raise an old board which has lain on top of leaves or grass a long time, you will find the round pellets of black fine dirt left there by the worms. The harvesters are too big to go into the robber ants' town to rout them out, Queen and all. So they go to the rubbish heap and get a whole mess of earthworm pellets. With these they stop up all the robbers' doorways. The robbers keep desperately digging out somewhere else but the harvesters keep plugging up the "leaks." After a while they slow down in the attack and the robbers, finding a chance, clear out as fast as their legs will carry them. Tired out and covered with dirt, they go away and for a time at least the harvesters once more enjoy peace.

If this might only be!

What if our homes were overrun as they were in Hamelin Town by thousands of rats with no pied piper to lead them away. Ant towns have a trouble much like that sometimes. The smallest kind of ant in the world is a thief and acts like a rat in the homes of larger ants. Just as the rat may have his hole in our cellar, the tiny thief ants have their holes in the earth so close to the bigger ants' rooms that they can tunnel in more easily than a rat gnaws his way under a door to steal our food. But the ant thieves are more terrible to have around than rats, for they steal the big ants' children. Children of other ants are their favorite food. Thousands of the tiny thieves creep into the nurseries sometimes and help themselves. The big ants chase them but cannot follow down their holes any more than we can rush down rat holes. Sometimes the thief ants turn and fight. A rat bite is very bad, but to big ants a thief ant's sting is worse. It is so poisonous that a big ant, stung, has convulsions and cannot defend itself from all the bites the thieves may give it. How badly such ants need pied pipers!

Another small-sized kind of ant enters the city of larger ants to beg rather than steal. They build their own town close by, like a suburb, and commute to the big town every day. Here, like gypsies who beg on our streets but give us pleasure by their very looks, by dancing or telling fortunes, these beggar ants offer a shampoo for a "handout." Meeting a big worker a beggar nimbly climbs upon its back and licks its head. This is a pleasure to the big ant and she brings up a drop of honeydew for the little stranger as you might take a coin from your purse to give a gypsy.

But there are many "out-of-town" visitors in

BEGGARS, BOOTLEGGERS, BANDITS

some ant cities which are not other kinds of ants but beetles and other insects. Some of these beetles look at first glance almost like ants. And they fool the workers who give them honeydew. For they have learned enough of the ant tap language to ask for it. Even as mosquitoes bother us, tiny mites pester ants and are very troublesome to be rid of. One kind of beetle earns its keep among the ants by eating the mites off them, to their delight.

There is a sort of pickpocket insect which lives among the ants. When honeydew gatherers are coming home it watches until it sees a stay-at-home worker ask for food. The two ants raise their faces to pass the honey one to the other. Just as the drop is halfway the pickpocket snatches it and dodges away. Thus the creature which doesn't work has stolen from two which do, robbing two pockets with one pick.

But this is nothing compared to the harm done by bootlegger beetles which peddle liquor among the ants. They ask for honeydew and get all they

THE WONDER WORLD OF ANTS

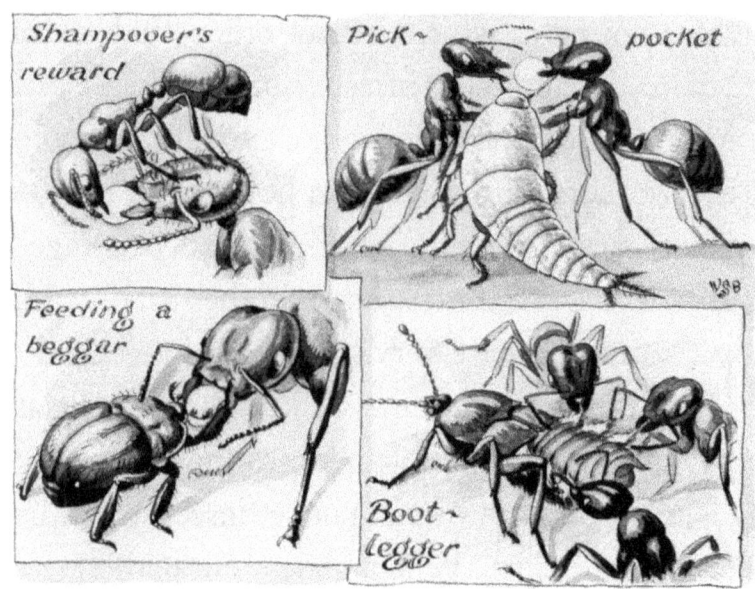

want because many of the ants are glad to pay for the liquor of the beetles. This liquor really makes them drunk. It oozes from the beetles' backs on sets of soft golden hairs, and the ants lap it eagerly. They forget to watch their eggs and babies. Then the bootlegger beetles steal and eat them. Not only that. The beetles lay their own eggs right in the ant city. The ants feed the beetle grubs and often forget to feed their own which grow to be useless citizens with no ambition to work. When enemy ants attack the city the drunkard ants save the beetles and beetle babies before they think of their own. After things go on this way for a time the whole city becomes so run down that it dies out, about as a tough mining town disappears when the gold rush is over.

There are many other kinds of insects which make trouble in the world of ants. But in our next chapter we shall see how one kind of ant enslaves another kind. Queens murder Queens and children are kidnaped to be raised in slavery.

SLAVE MAKERS

HERE in America we make railroad tunnels right through mountains, we sink deep mines for coal and metals, and we dig long subways for traveling underground. In and out of these we swarm like ants. But we never hollow out entire cities and live our whole lives underground. Yet in North Africa there are tribes of people known as Troglodytes who have lived in cities far below the surface of the earth for hundreds of years. Their homes are carved in soft but solid rock thirty feet or more beneath the ground at the bottom of great dry wells some seventy feet across. Through long slanting tunnels they leave the level ground to reach these homes whose doors open around the inside of the wells. Along the tunnel walls are hollowed barns for goats, donkeys, chickens, and camels. Down be-

SLAVE MAKERS

side the rooms in which they live are storerooms for food and valuables. It is all very much like an orderly ant town, sheltered from harsh weather and from their savage enemies.

In the surrounding deserts wander half wild Arabs who sometimes try to raid the ant-like city, steal the food and carry captured women off as slaves. They are not often able to rob such well protected people as the Troglodytes, but further south they have much more success. For ages they have gone down into damper lands where grass and jungles grow to capture Negroes living there.

THE WONDER WORLD OF ANTS

The Negroes cannot defend their grass-roofed houses as easily as Troglodytes protect their homes, though they fight most bravely. It is against the law to carry on slavery in Africa today. But so much of it is still so wild and hard to patrol that many secret Arab slave raiders still ply their terrible trade. Many people are killed and those caught are taken away and sold.

Fortunately this is not a very common custom any more among mankind, but among some kinds of ants it goes on all the time. There are various tribes of fighting ants who cannot do a good day's work and simply have to have a lot of slaves to get along. Perhaps the finest of these warrior ants are those called Amazons. They are named for tribes of warrior women who lived in olden times, females famous for ferocious fighting. Ancient Greeks wrote of their deeds and drew lively pictures of them in battle.

Amazon ants are just as fierce as human Amazons or slave-raiding Arabs. Their great crescent

SLAVE MAKERS

jaws are sharp as curving Arab scimitars. They can stab through the hard head of an enemy ant in one cruel crunch. They make slaves of certain hard-working dark gray ants whose cities they attack. The swarthy Arabs make slaves of all black people they can capture, men, women and children. But the brown Amazon ants only take the children of the dark gray ants after conquering the grown-ups. The babies, stolen in their cocoons, grow up to work in the city of the Amazons, and think of it as home, never having known another. There are many dark gray slaves of all ages in an Amazon city. Perhaps they don't mind their lot, for it is their nature to work hard and they were kidnaped while still all wrapped and sleeping in cocoons. They never saw the cruel battle that was waged to save them.

I must tell you how an Amazon city gets started. Since no Amazon (and certainly not the Queen) ever does a stroke of work, except to lick herself and primp, there must be slaves right at the beginning. When a new Amazon Queen flies to the earth after her wedding, she doesn't look for a place to dig a room and go to work at laying eggs and caring for them. She goes looking for a city of the dark gray ants. Presently she finds one and walks toward it slowly, attracting as little attention as possible. As she gets nearer to the entrance dark gray workers stop her. They don't like Amazon ants. Perhaps her kind of people have made trouble for them many times. Ants remember. But the dark gray people have mild natures, it takes a lot to make them fighting mad. They may take hold of the stranger and try to keep her from going into their city, but very often she manages to get past them. She finally finds her way into the chamber of the dark gray Queen herself. These Amazon Queens must be very tactful. For now she actually makes friends with her hostess and sits with her in the royal chamber.

Then one morning the dark gray nurses come in to freshen things up and find their Queen lying

SLAVE MAKERS

dead, stabbed through her regal head! There sits the Amazon in her place. The dark grays take their Queen to the cemetery and perhaps because they do not understand just how this all has happened, they do not try to oust the Amazon but accept her as the new Queen. They raise all the old Queen's babies which now have lost their mother and, side by side with these, care for all the little Amazons hatching from the murderess's eggs. No more dark gray eggs are laid of course, only Amazons, fewer and fewer dark gray ants, more and more Amazons. The dark gray ants do all the work. They care for the Amazon Queen and her children, dig new rooms and keep the place clean, go out hunting and dairying, and feed the Amazons every one.

The work finally gets too hard. More slaves are needed. A raid is planned. Amazon scouts go out in all directions, seeking cities of the dark gray ants. When they find one they study all its openings and the lay of the land about it. Then they return to lead the raiding warriors. Leaving a strong guard at home to keep the slaves in hand, the Amazon army sets forth, all keeping close together following the scouts. Now they reach the dark grays' city. They halt. Dark gray ants are gathering about the entrances, worried, and they do not want a fight. They have always worked, not practiced fighting like these Amazons. Their jaws are spades, not swords.

Suddenly the Amazons attack! The dark grays grapple desperately. The children must be saved! Everywhere ants are fighting, biting, rolling in

SLAVE MAKERS

the dust, three on one, four on two, or "man to man." Legs come off, feelers break, soon heads leave bodies, the jaws still biting bravely. Some ants go crazy with pain and roll on the ground biting themselves. Now a dark gray, surrounded by Amazons, squirts poison from its hinder end. It kills one Amazon but they squirt back and finish the dark gray. The Amazons are winning. They have gotten into some of the holes. Quickly some of the dark grays rush to rescue the children. They are going to make a dash for it. While others still fight off the Amazons, they try to carry the cocoons out of the city to safe hiding. But the Amazons fight even harder now. They are swifter than the dark gray ants. They catch many of the fleeing cocoon carriers. An Amazon places her sharp jaws on a dark gray's head and hesitates. "Drop that cocoon!", she seems to be saying. But the dark gray hangs on unwisely. Pinch! Into its head go the Amazon daggers. Home goes the Amazon, carrying the cocoon of a dark gray future slave. Now Amazons are coming out of the city carrying more cocoons which they have found. The battle still goes on, the unhappy dark grays following the kidnapers, trying to make them let the children go. But they cannot keep up with the swift-running raiders and give it up at last, tired and beaten, many badly wounded. Back they straggle through the battlefield where dark gray ants and Amazons lie dead on every hand.

This doesn't sound so very decent, does it? It is even worse to think that people sometimes act the same. But in the next and last chapter of this

SLAVE MAKERS

book you will read of ants which make war not only upon every other kind of ant they meet, but on every living thing they come upon, even attacking people and driving them out of their homes.

ARMY ANTS

ABOUT fifteen hundred years ago there came into Europe, from the East, a fierce tribe of military people called the Huns. They were of the Mongol race, with swarthy yellow skins, almond eyes, and straight black hair. The Huns were horsemen and they swept over Asia and Europe, conquering every people in their path. Even the Romans with their great cities and trained armies had to pay them tribute. This savage people built no towns and cities of their own, but lived by plundering those who did, tak-

ARMY ANTS

ing their food and whatever else they wanted, and moving on. Back in Mongolia, even today, there are wild mounted tribes of men who do not wander so far but have the same fierce ways as the Huns of old.

In the world of ants there is a similar people living mostly in the tropics, who make no cities nor anything else but war. It is their only intention to kill and eat everything they come upon. Nothing is safe, from single insects or entire cities of other types of ants, to men and even elephants. They are called driver, wandering, or army ants. Like the Huns, they spread terror before them. Animals know they are coming before people do, for they smell them first. And the smell is that of rotten meat. These ants, unlike other kinds, do not like sweet food. They care for meat only, and the parts of victims which they do not eat at once they carry with them. In warm countries this soon gets bad. No wonder animals smell their marching millions from afar.

THE WONDER WORLD OF ANTS

And they do march. Moving in close order, some of their armies are hundreds of yards long and a good many feet wide, each ant touching the next. Millions of ants! A moving murder-carpet! In front and along the flanks go the bigger soldiers ready for the attack and keeping the lines in order. Between them the smaller soldiers go. They not only help fight whatever they come upon, but carry all the baby soldiers and the eggs of their Queen. She is there too, moving along somewhere near the middle of the mass. If there are any young royalty they are with the rest.

On they go, marching, killing, eating. Other insects try to crawl to safety, but some of the soldiers crawl after them, up trees, down holes, anywhere. Grasshoppers are so terrified they forget to jump and are torn to pieces. In Africa, when the ant Huns come to a native village, they drive the people out of their homes and eat everything that remains. In they swarm and up the walls to the grass roofs where they catch every flea, louse,

ARMY ANTS

cockroach, centipede and lizard. Into mouse and ratholes they run and nothing there escapes. This is good house cleaning but if a person were helpless and left lying indoors they would "clean him up" too. Only his bones would be left in a very short time.

Sometimes white men in the tropics stand all four legs of their beds in pails of kerosene or vinegar. Through this the ants cannot swim to crawl up the posts. A person is safe as long as he stays in the bed, unless part of a blanket touches the floor or unless the ants jump upon him from the ceiling. Unless, unless— It is better to leave home for a few hours even though in the middle of the night, the time often chosen by African army ants for their raids.

A man must turn his cattle, hogs or other animals loose to save them and hope they will come back in the morning. If he builds fires about the animal pens the ants may be turned aside. But if he does not get them built before they arrive it is very little use.

Out in the forest the wild animals are all forced to flee. For nothing can stand being bitten in one thousand places one moment, ten thousand places the next moment, and a hundred thousand more places in no time. The most poisonous snake, the fiercest lion, the biggest, toughest elephant, and every other beast both large and small, must get out of the way. In South America even the anteater cannot eat them fast enough to keep from being eaten. Birds must take to the air and ferocious crocodiles must slide down the river banks into the water.

THE WONDER WORLD OF ANTS

Though fire sometimes stops the army ants, water does not. Even where men cannot cross a stream in times of flood the army ants are able. They gather themselves into a great ball as big as a bushel, with the Queen and her brood in the middle. Then they roll into the water and float along till they come again to solid ground. Here they re-form their ranks and march on. If it is only a little trickle of water to be crossed some of them form a bridge of themselves and the others march across it.

Of course these insect armies rest sometimes. They make their camp with their own bodies. Again they become a living ball, this time perhaps in a hollow tree. The center of the ball they form like a room and there rests the Queen. There too, through tunnels formed by others, the smaller soldiers bring her brood of eggs and babies and the meat they have not eaten on the march. So rests the fearsome army till time for a fresh foray. You would not expect them to have any friends.

ARMY ANTS

Yet there are certain wasps and odd beetles which look much like them and go with them everywhere. They have enlisted in the ant army and eat their share of captured food.

If the ants I used to watch (when I was a boy and wanted to go to Africa) had been army ants instead of the kind that live in cooler countries, I wouldn't have been able to lie in the grass without being eaten alive. But I should like to see them now in their own far off lands, just as much as I'd like to see the big wild animals and dark wild people, wouldn't you?

www.ingramcontent.com/pod-product-compliance
Lightning Source LLC
Chambersburg PA
CBHW080523110426
42742CB00017B/3212